maroon choreography

maroon cho

BLACK OUTDOORS: Innovations in the Poetics of Study
A series edited by J. Kameron Carter and Sarah Jane Cervenak

** ography**   fahima ife

Duke University Press   *Durham and London*   2021

© 2021 Duke University Press
All rights reserved
Designed by Courtney Leigh Richardson
Typeset in Whitman and Canela by Copperline Book Services

Library of Congress Cataloging-in-Publication Data
Names: Ife, Fahima, [date] author.
Title: Maroon choreography / Fahima Ife.
Other titles: Black outdoors.
Description: Durham : Duke University Press, 2021. |
Series: Black outdoors | Includes index.
Identifiers: LCCN 2020046222 (print)
LCCN 2020046223 (ebook)
ISBN 9781478013341 (hardcover)
ISBN 9781478014256 (paperback)
ISBN 9781478021568 (ebook)
Subjects: LCGFT: Poetry. | Essays.
Classification: LCC PS3609.F35 M37 2021 (print) |
LCC PS3609.F35 (ebook) | DDC 818/.609—dc23
LC record available at https://lccn.loc.gov/2020046222
LC ebook record available at https://lccn.loc.gov/2020046223

Frontispiece and chapter opening art: Photo by fahima ife.

Publication of this book is supported by Duke University Press's
Scholars of Color First Book Fund.

for   poet **Taylor Johnson**   who reminds me to listen

stay knowing that if they get this dance, there might be something wrong.
stay knowing that if something is only to be gotten, we
might all be doing something wrong.

—**taisha paggett**

contents

a prefatory note   ix

recrudescence   1

porous aftermath   15

nocturnal work   51

maroon choreography   79

coda   93
anindex   117

a prefatory note

Everything in Maroon Choreography is occurring (or has occurred) in what Fred Moten, in Black and Blur, calls "the native fugue-state of being-composed," and it is a sense of being-and-not-being-composed, of moving through a series of disembodied lapses, outside any sense of bodily identities, that I move through and work to unravel through this work. The poems, poetic fragments, and lyrical essay in this collection presuppose a way out (of captivity, indebtedness, ecological ruin) by way of minimalist errantry, by way of refusal.

Creatively, methodologically, and theoretically, Maroon Choreography is preoccupied with anachoreography. Anachoreography is a recursive practice of refusal. I refuse the choreographed apparatuses of coloniality, its methodologies, its origin stories, its naming rituals, and its movements. To move elsewhere and practice otherwise, I retrace my breath, loop back, and move with the opaque air. In the unseen, unknown expanse of blackness, I move inside the palimpsest of what exists prior, or beside us. Anachoreography is the feral spirit of *study, waywardness, tarrying, ritual, practice, rehearsal, shoal, ceremony, series, rematriation, wake, duration, intimacy, pause,* and *refusal*—given to us in the poiesis of black studies, ecological studies, performance studies, affect studies, and indigenous studies. If dance is the city's mother tongue, as Fred Moten says, then what secret lives inside the city, in us, before the city, as us, before the clearing, inside air?

I began with a series of questions on the mythic human body, questions about proprioceptive sense limits, how a body moves in space, how we make sense of our movement in space, and how to expand our flesh limits. Alexis Pauline Gumbs, in Dub, questions historical biopolitics by looking back at Sylvia Wynter's work and asking, what happens if what we consider as our blood lineage is simply a matter of paint? Through *Maroon Choreography* I ask, what if the entire narrative of enslavement and settler colonialism is just echolalia?

Nominal predispositions, naming rituals, linger in terms of race, gender, sexuality, class, ability, age, and so forth, are reanimated through an ongoing sense of self-regard, or relentless pride in looking back at, of having moved through, of being connected to, history. What if our sense of inherited subjectivity is sound? What if the reality we think we inhabit is nothing more than oscillation? Years into the future (now), will we look back at it, our inherited names, narratives, our bloodlines, hold on to them, refuse to change as everything around us changes all for the sake of belonging, of grounding ourselves in presumed subjectivity?

To refuse a biopolitical and sociohistorical patina, I ask, what undocumented black indigenous knowledges emerged in the seventeenth century on Turtle Island, and how do those knowledges persist in our contemporary air? Though it does not answer, *Maroon Choreography* moves inside the pneumatic feeling of fleeing in seventeenth-century black indigenous escape and lingers.

The seven years I spent at work on *Maroon Choreography*, in meticulous study, in solitude, in dispersal, in depression, are the years I spent cauterizing my relationship with this colonial language and its obsession with documenting the world and its bodies. Seven years ago I began studying the bureaucratic origins of writing and contemporary performances of poetry and poetics. My preoccupation with language and literacy is inspired by my maternal grandparents' inherited illiteracy. The fact that my grandparents, born during the Great Depression in the United States South, were made to work the land in this country and not develop a way with words has material consequences I continue to exist within. The uterine cancer my grandmother, Levada, experienced in her thirty-sixth year, a circumstance she survived for thirty more years before death, is likely a result of years of agricultural field labor, touching/breathing the toxic air of pesticides, picking the toxic food someone else would eat. The series of heart attacks my grandfather, Lucius, experienced in his sixty-first year (before his death in that same year) is likely the result of years of hard field and steel mill labor, and alcohol, caffeine, and nicotine addiction simply to make it through. I got so far inside the history of English language, orality and literacy, so far inside the imposition of black bodies within the documentary lineage of the written word, I lost my ability to participate, lost whatever imposed socializations, whatever norms, modes of group etiquette, expectations for research, I might have imitated or drawn upon in the past when I still believed academic writing was anything other than an irrefutable matter of money.

André Lepecki, in *Exhausting Dance*, equates choreography with the commands of writing, so a "disciplined body" is one that moves according to captivity's expectations for expression—bound in solipsism, in forced submission, the (dead) master's voice on loop in the background. Levada and Lucius are two relatives in a long line—all the way back through the eighteenth-century agrarian (United States) South—of (black) farmers, workers, stewards of the land and field. The people I claim as familiar by way of a mythical grand blood lineage were field laborers, who worked the fields, for hundreds of years, without proper compensation or nourishment, whose lives were cut short by labor. This is the choreography of their external bodies, not interior.

Insofar as I could question the otherwise entanglements of movement and writing, I began to search for another mode of movement, one not reliant upon choreography as rule or dictated orientation, but a movement born in wildness, in fugitivity, in refusal. Inside the academy there are fields and bodies, conversations on how those fields and bodies remain in isolation, and expectations to argue on bodies within fields. There are single-disciplinary-field trajectories, and then there are radical creative-intellectual amalgamations, the interdisciplines, the cross-disciplines—the undisciplined—the matter that moves us beyond the academy, beyond the fields. *Maroon Choreography* is an attempt to document black study as something otherwise, some wiser configuration other than an argument.

If there is a traceable beginning to this work, before I moved to Louisiana, before I traveled to and lived briefly in Paris, it emerged in the sixteen years I spent in quiet study with my grandmother while she was alive. Levada is dead, but she is not gone. She is air. Anachoreography, as method and practice, involves opening up to, stammering, and moving again inside our quiet, entangled, pneumatic intimacies. The quiet I continue to share with my grandmother, in the two decades after her death, is supplemented by extensive study between and across multiple fields and nonfields.

After and at the same time as *Maroon Choreography* I am trying to enliven a prolonged discussion on the preternatural intimacy I share with my dead grandmother, on one level, and cultivate a hauntological practice that perhaps might yield a theory on movement, on another level. I want to get more precise in practicing and articulating the imprecise (im)materiality of our shared air, the nonfungible porousness I share with Levada, a woman who could not read or write in her time here but who continues reading and writing through me.

Maroon Choreography is ongoing, a series of works in ecological black study deriving from a series of still-unfolding questions on air and movement. In this work and the work to come I ask, what unregulated qualities of air flourish in our global ecologies? What otherwise porous ecosystems emerge, or do we have access to, by way of deep listening? In *Maroon Choreography* my primary interlocutor, my unseen collaborator, is my dead maternal grandmother, Levada Harris. Though she died twenty-two years ago, we continue to share cosmic intimacy, we continue to study, and we continue to move together. My practice in *Maroon Choreography* is an attempt to collaborate with my grandmother's spirit to shape knowledge, to practice developing a theory informed by the knowledges she could not express while she was here, as flesh, among the living. Yet *Maroon Choreography* is not about my grandmother. The world inside *Maroon Choreography* attempts to move outside the blackness-as-enslavement narrative, to move inside a collective black interior by way of breathing.

In the pages that follow are three sections of poems and a lyrical essay. The poems, "Recrudescence" (a relevé in eleven parts), "Porous Aftermath" (a fugue in thirty-three parts), and "Nocturnal Work" (an improvisation in twenty-two parts), I see as a long recursive dance. The poems encounter our ecstatic air and move in it. The lyrical essay, "Maroon Choreography," is a long unbroken paragraph on form. The essay discusses place, space, time, and study—or where I was, what I experienced, and what I read—as the poems formed themselves through me. In lieu of a formal bibliography, notes, or index, the book closes with an errant coda, an experimental entanglement of all the texts I read, or otherwise engaged, in the process of working on this book. The coda entangles the titles and authors of works in a series of formations, or multiple progressions on each page, and omits publication details. I include this material not only as a means of accounting for what I covered, but also as a way to symbolically represent the philosophic grounds I was so immersed within for all the years I spent at work on this project, and how I imagine those works in a sort of ongoing creative cross-pollination with one another, how it all fades back to the nothingness of blackness. An anindex, a poetic index, follows the coda. The anindex references the muted *mu* concepts as they exist within the pages of this book. *Mu* as in Nathaniel Mackey's wandering band of jazz artists, *mu* as in the nothing space of Zen Buddhism, *mu* as in the words whose utterance most amuses my tongue. The anindex defies alphabetical impulse, instead offers a final procession of seven sets of words, to insinuate another variation on movement throughout this book.

This work will work only if you, friend, are open. Words are merely words unless we are open. To move deep inside the life of these poems, create an opening. Read the pieces, slow, in the pace of the life of each poem. Listen close. Read this work three times: once in a linear progression, from what we understand as beginning to end, then again from the middle outward, and a third time in whatever way you choose. Pause. Pause in between moving from one page to the next. Pause at the end of a line. Pause whenever you encounter white space. Pause according to punctuation. Pause to match your breath to the pace of aeration in the work. Pause in stillness and breathe. Read this work outside under the open air of sky, under the breadth of trees, in the air of things. Read this work with friends, out loud, preferably while listening to some sort of avant-garde instrumental music (low in the background); pause in between reading to dance, or whatever it is you call it when you lose yourself in movement. Come together, in whatever creative configuration necessary, to talk about the work, talk about the inscrutable space of air, in between words, what is not spoken as the words themselves are spoken. Ask more of what we make of communing, of coming, of dispersing, of moving, of learning alongside one another. Arrive and arrive again in communion—the only desire I have for this work.

or was it afterlife

gravity in the green of

scrawls against their droughts

the wet word

ectoplasm

a glint of silver slivers

or subduction

of a grave

blood was not their blood

glistens them succulent

igneous brine it hollows them

cadence of the night

it cauls them

outside an orifice

want listens   to need lust

as blackness

glistens and slips inside
night's moist opening

listens to night
call light to life memory

until sentience it moves us

{   }

exhaustive

after midnight

what heat
we were hinged as

was always with us

{ *queeribbeanness* }

was it crude we strolled into
or some other unasked for

out and into
emanation

no the blurring of ~~queer~~ fugitive fucking
nothing normal fucking
everything ~~black~~

night glistens

        sinuous

    and sensuous

        as night is

            singular

        transfiguration breathes

in ascendance

        calls desire

no name   outside itself

            a feeling roots

    an idea hollows

            a concept

maroon as air

is green

this old feeling

when anamnesis

and nothing

drifts

in a tar pit

a name is

{ abstraction }

or occluded

at the summoning

of sentience

of the marsh

of the trench

on the precipice of

the end of money

an opening

green as green it greens

drifting

                parabotanical
digression

or evasive

on edge

of transfiguration

obsidian or gloss

obfuscation

absence airs

presence airs

time it

weights

presence digs

abstraction in ether

digs expanse with

consents to the touch

of movement

as air

aerates chthonic pressure

until quiver

        a buck is broken

    a sense is buck

       a bend is black

              tremulous

           antegrammatical

              as in flesh

       or enfleshment

      antebotanical
  as *mahamudra*
        endobotanical

                  as sky

                  is moonless

porous aftermath

•/

    they were seven a woman a man
        five children dancing
            to liquid

    edge between plantation and fecund
        swamp { they are black and red
            pulsating

    appetite at midnight at thieving
        hour they are drifting
            on bruised legs

    and nearly failed lungs mammalian
        wandering a densely
            lined tree edge }

    between plantation memory and
        cosmic impulse they were
            bodies then

•//

    their tear-stained cheeks and aching backs their
        sounding feet ruined from
            rigid cane

    all seven ageless copper cortex
        on the edge of ambu-
            latory

    nothing and everything in bayou
        winter bodies restless
            tidewater

•///

    their fibrous connective tissues like
        muscle and bone and hair
           make them kin

    entangle them as difference
        in tongue in expression
           in sound wave

    until their music becomes cosmic
        more than colony more
           than mother

    { not gender not sex } serpentine as
        river runs sinuous
           lithe and lock

•—

as bioluminescent as the
      work of loving their bones
          arthritic

calcified flesh matter hardened as
      blue-black time signature
          a problem

not their own { taken } stolen made as
      leaves their flesh { opens }
          as they roam

wayward as naught other than poly
      as air inside tarries
          chromatic

•////

{ they were porous } branded fleur-de-lis
        floral luminescent
                property

they were flesh then with tissue problems
        marooned and colored as
                property

their arms rendered gold and sugar and
        rice and indigo and
                property

they were money then indebted to
        time owed until time erased
                property

{ they are porous } refusing themselves
        gloss in the spiral of
                property

•\

when their lungs reach capacity
      they weep not blue wailing but
           in quiet

they weep in an inside space slipping
      where no sound is uttered
           dead quiet

they die { kill a part of themselves } so
      they might live forever
           fugitive

•\\

when their lungs reach capacity
        they bend on all fours slip
              in winter

they crawl a copper-colored ground as
        sky calls their other names
              furtive names

•\\\

    as their flesh tongues ethereal bone
            they come together as
                    precision

    tantric as the wind blows they tremble
            ecstatic as midnight
                  departure

    no more flesh and blood and calcium
            no more joint tissue ache
                  not water

—•

ethereal as horizon blues they
    communicate as
        liquid edge

without tongues and lips and vocal cords
    tongue mother become breath
        as air comes

when they come together in rhythm
    they are seven no more
        inscription

•\\\\

{ they eat names } ethnocentric gender
        biological sex-
                ism's land

what constellations held them as
        human incarnation
               it drains them

in bayou winter they leave names like
        race or would or raced
               ritual-

istic amalgam and wooden juke
        { opaque as a wet room
               in autumn }

they roast names homegrown categories
        apex predator as
               human child

{ they ate names } *bambara* and *choctaw*
        as *culebra* as warm
               bulbancha

•|

    insofar as sound is air they are
          blue-black moaning using
                gut as flute

    { city tongue } mother tongue { movement tree }
          first imagined in as
              belly of

    a ship in as :: cello :: of a tree
          or human marketplace
              as fusain

    grapheme fades { quiet crescendo }
          it's the touch of the out-
              side that hails

    them { insofar as frequency is
          oracle } they are *mu*
              or fuchsia

    fusarium apparatus
          fertile fermentation
              feral dream

•||

etymology made them design
 made them blackindian
  and maroon

made them names they did not call themselves
 like divided in two
  or gender

•|||

names not taken { but given } not owned
:: possessed :: records not blank
but bloodstained

{ they eat names } etched in oil-slick vinyl
red as ink as feather
{ desire

wanders } in black dawn as cicada
comes all night bold they come
{ *quilombo* }

wet names { melancholy } as snow as
how they bend { as time } blurs
how they leave

• — |

insofar as sound is air they are
        poor in spirit { poor as }
              breathing

the breeze as earth matter pollinates
        the wildest parts are black
              like breathing

their lungs grow into something other
        than windpipe { cosmic flute }
              when they dance

on the other side of sugarcane
        a cosmic riddle grass
                is burning

fertile as the land is black as the
        food is black as the air
                is black as

the word is black as the way is black
        as the earth is black as
                mirth is black

•||||

bitter apparatus inflamed flesh
      fossil fuel field matter
           they were that

{ estrus } emanation or open
      hour made of moonlight
           :: slips outside ::

alive outside the line off the line
      tangential to the name
         outside time

|•

    vehement in bayou winter they are
        portal between here and
            brass ether

    signal between spore and star matter
        opaque as nothingness
            :: lungs open ::

    hidden as seven human echoes
        alive in *bas du fleuve*
            lungs heaving

    quiet as dense copper cortex
        or aerial trees they
            ground and

    leave as air fornicates an open
        out run fear's frequency
            wayward as

    ecstatic wind moves as nothing as
        seventeen seventy-seven
            intimate

    series of secret runs in winter
        porous human { poor as
            blackness }

||•

    insofar as rain is balm is ache
            is flood is flooded
                is fluid

    is torment is tempestuous is
          always need always need
                sweet black mire

    precise time signature chorus cries
          calcifying is not
                our release

    water is { want in the tidewater }
          is midnight ache is drought
                in need of

    nimbostratus clouds and hurricane
        moons all three slippery
            and porous

    liquid edge is grieving grieving
          summoning { at midnight
              something dies }

III•

    not a single human being but
            multiple gathered
                  serial

    they live as fecund as movement { not
            owned } not propertied
                  not possessed

    or dispossessed { not ownership }
            they deny a single
                  existence

    { homeless } someplace meteor showered
            wooden loam covered black
                  resolving

    not to be a slave to be wayward
            not documented
                  sacred swathe

..\

    they are resolving not to be a
        slave or be a human
            or solve flesh

    to tongue dance to move without form to
        move ephemeral as
            moonlight to

    tongue in open tidewaters to wake
        mother to dream to bend
            branches low

    to slump to surrender to offer
        to worship to dance to
            loss tree line

    to tongue { out mother tongue } without form
        bone to assemblage to
            loss flesh

    porous aftermath to agitate
        in bayou winter to
            tongue to live ::

..\\

    on another side of sugarcane
           { they gloss } cross narrow
                  chthonic bridge

    pushed outward from inside out { glisten
           low } slide inside tree-lined
                  island

    insofar as mound swallows them
           broken they replenish
                tendentious

    earth swallowed and alienated
           as air or { as nothing }
                insofar

    as their dearly beloved movement
           is shadowed withdrawn and
                out of touch

..\\\

    here they are nameless bodyspirit
            only not woman not
                  man not sex

    not gender not child not father not
        adult not mother not
            daughter not

    son not nephew not niece not female
        not male not intersex
            { not scripted }

    not pronoun not name not label not
        capital not human
            { not captive }

    not master not mastered not mistress
        not misery not form
            :: abstraction ::

••\\\\

    poor as tambourine syncopation
            they live as cicada
                  upside ground

    beside plantation lines in line as
            spirit { warm breeze greets autumn
                  fog passage }

    tree frog leaps between cocoon and sky
            as bodies become no
                  body no

    trace of human inhabitation
            rhythmic as dense earth
                  succulent

..|

    seven androgynous twin spirit
        ethnobotanical
            ascendance

    now there are no ways of dividing
        seven no meaningless
            assignments

    no records of names like color like
        religious bifurcation
            financial

    circumstance at birth was your mama
        a slave { did she run off
            at midnight? }

••‖

{ not body } pneumatic declension
        seven runners open
                aimless

{ open } as quiet saturation
        fugitive as ythmic
                refusal

{ open } as improvised transitions
        they come together
                as they run

{ not body } energy of seven
        dancers measureless
                as air

their pneumatic polychromatic
        dance undocumented
                as air

••|||

a winter breeze blows a naked tree
        no more tree than dancer
                tranquilo

as the leaves scatter { the body leaves }
    tranquilo   *tranquilo*
          relax now

malleable in the flicker dream
    tranquilo   *tranquilo*
        as air

••||||

not genetic afterlives after
        slavery not that negro
                spiritual

of spirit as pneuma of spirit
        not solipsistic
                afterlives

of schism :: ism and ist left earth
        no more genetic blood
                saga { gone }

|••

    in incubation they move as wind
            mercurial séance
                to fly as

    tree is a naked dancer cosmic
            its branches a lost arm
                a leg loose

    not inflammation not sugar blues
            not malt gluten gut rot
                not blood sick

    not sciatic nerve { vexation } not blue
            not sugar overdose
                not cane sick

    not flesh not barbecue precision
            not malignant echo
                not flesh

‖••

      when no one runs the trees { at night they
            dance } move in quiet
                  as spirit

      flee the porousness of older skins
            as open wind { *tranquilo*
                  tranquilo }

      not bitter apparatus not bone
            not nitrogen flesh womb
                  not seven

      not human { energy of cypress }
            spirits in dancer's pose
                  not human

      supple branch legs thrust open and out
            cypress maybe cypress
                  naked now

      not human energy of live oak
            spirits in dancer's pose
                  branches out

|||••

unrecorded undocumented
        unkempt more than blue and
                black and black

and blue { also polychromatic
        saturation } heir
                to nothing

||||••

a green note pierces a wounded ship
        into oblivion
                black echo

chamber troubles their chromatic
        troubled { origin } as
              a thing to

run from and as and into :: madness ::
        a black echo chamber
              resounds

a broken branch remembers quiet
        cracks under the weight of
              transition

...

    not runaway slave not fugitive
            not bound not resolving
                to not be

    a single breath at fuchsia hour
            as wind summons a black
                moon at dawn

    a child becomes pneumatic dance
            becomes fuchsia ether
                becomes *was*

    not runaway slave not fugitive
            failing to resolve life's
                blood matter

    to not resolve to be a human
            not seven fugitives
                only trees

•|•

on the other side of sugarcane
        old debt { is rolled } they owe
            no time or

space as cypress { as mourning } as the
        money { sweetens out } as
            human ache

blue as maple { grass } a cosmic run
        as venomous as
            cryptic haunt

or *duende* wind { cosmic flower } as
        cannabis sativa
            is sugar

nocturnal work

with   C. G. Jung, Fred Moten, Édouard Glissant, Taylor Johnson, Dionne Brand, Christopher Gilbert, Gwendolyn Brooks, Nathaniel Mackey, Henry Dumas, Sebastian Clark, Rae Armantrout, Danielle Vogel, Malidoma Patrice Somé, Nathanaël, Simone White, Evie Shockley, Nicole Terez Dutton, and Cole Swensen

anamnesis, amanuensis

      emptiness cuts our collective fugue state
      cuts through corrugated banality

wills the unnecessary metallic grounds of existence

uneasiness wills its way around my
swollen tongue

      the extract
      i make my language out of
      so i might speak to you

            as
              frequency

            as the music { it crawls inside }
            moves in close and this feeling

            could be called desire
            were i alive

            were i living
            the most sublime

            { in the history of escape }

shamanism

no it is not common
what burns in me
this bitter earth
the more i polish it
the more lustrous i become
outside where i left my shoes
in the cool morning gray
there was no end
to the precarity
in a connection
i became
what is the
name?

auto—

what makes a petro-
chemical addict in
want of an antagonist?
the need for air
a grip
once   in the
green-scented myopia
of generalized melancholia
i watched my sensitive body
fight itself   for seven
burning years before
i remembered
the word
no

a matter more malleable than meaning

{ i began to live exclusively in the realm of music }

inside a hollow tree
there were many secrets

succulence that could make you invisible
transform the body

into anything you wished

i was not dead but close

lost between flesh
and intimation

a coming of (and into)

recurrence   the transition
slanting

a granular motion inside

the chromium slanting
recurrence

a muscular twitch inside the earth
its contractions

{ or peristalsis }

a night in which my spirit cowers

i quiver the delirious succulent air and fear to sleep as one fears a great whole

haunted   they say   believing my spirit haunted by its vertigo

it can appear in human form   but is most often elsewhere

the speed of darkness   the silver resonant humming

in the depths words run transparent from my mouth

and almost find the edge of subduction the into

that was music said: *be alive   be willing*

how little i commit myself to living

lost inside the hole of naught

aporia

{ the one who runs the night }
    what am i?

       { indigenous not citizen }
          what native?

{ black shoal } { black wake }
    what wellness?

       { light to pass to light }
       what biomyth?

       { ambulatory in the night }
       what knowledge?

         { somnambulism }
    what reason?

{   }
    what death?

~~seven generations of labor~~
    what secret?

       { the depths
    the depths }

an aspect of fire

lilac fume someplace astral

      stolen
or was it gone?

we were deracination

unfielded

to run a relay
transmit a baton

pass on
pass it on between us

it is not reality we were in
as much as portal

{ cerebral helix }

the city bleeds

      in a package of minutes
      there is this we—

the blood of a new place drank in their faces as a new moon

{ memory } { contains the ambiguities }
{ as air chemicals of its subjection }

      { in the black } and outside { a headless
      body dances to rhythms }

      { a strange cosmic vibration }

{ a tremor of song }{ the rivulets of }{ a young mind }

{ night } { is a lost } { and ungrounded thing }
      { the beauty of night is haunting }

      { the weight
           of the moon's beams }

           { into the depths of ecstatic red }

                  { of contemplative largesse }
           { the depths } { of years of deaths }

      { a timeless voice } { *oh beauty* }

{ seven times they looked around }
      { in seven different directions }

           { and there was no voice owner }
           { but the weight of the moon }
           { imposed on air } { a ritual }

           { to bear the acres or fall on their heads }

means of evasion

for breakfast i ate a bowl
of purple tentacles
while they were still alive
and undulating
as if my arm
or a bundle
of my woolen hair
had fallen inside
the orifice before me
and because
no one else
was present
i ate myself
then i became
a lilac blade of grass
a whole series of them
an impossible field
of purple grass
writhing in the wind
an entanglement of species
smoking as a woodwind
inside the empire
of still
people run
on all fours
as if in imitation
of our four-legged cousins
close to the ground
they catapult
their flesh
across
the intersections
they leap
and become
the last note of a clarinet

last week i died
under a black sky
its clouds
a swirling mass
of fuchsia
i died
and because
no one else
was present
i broke out
as an oud

post-acid

instead there was a white light
a mountain   a mounting

were it green a ground would open
were it fungus a digression

we stand in many doorways at once

our bones have no need for flesh
but this hunger

       transitive as the night

transcendence comes after cannabis
after psilocybin   after acid

   after   reality stops

   after   ruby lay cradled
                  dead

she got sick and died like everyone
bruised as rural lust

   after   it was eaten

the city that made a desire of me
broke under the weight of tenancy

we communicate together in a language that does not speak

but understood perfectly

we plunge into the negative
ecstasy of radio

an enriching emptiness
a resonating quiet

it is not weightlessness
we are in

as much as channel
ephemeral connecting space

the ecstasy of communication
now an obscene gesture

our sacred grounds
(was it ever?)

is no longer secret

we want our
hidden

glistening back

and simultaneously
it is disappearing

our ineffable
blackness

{   }

the word is free
but we are not

fleurs sauvages

maroon as air
is delicate
feels as
green

when
anamnesis
and soul
airs

afterlife
moves
propagates

a green
soul
airs

and
air

metanoia

you wept   a humid grave

vibration of the earth fuchsia

edges of the depths divine

intoxication was it madness

or   somnambulant

a child at age seven

hears spirits

the coming of darkness informed us it was time to join the circle

as if there were continuous explosions
and each one released
an immense force field
that took hold of the universe
my body became quiet
my body became
a thin tube
of translucent glass
i began to think of time
{ as a swathe }   a red grain
my body was now alive
and so was the whole bundle
i began to think of body
as   { an absence }
my body became multitudinous
as the ground is vertiginous
no longer reliant
on gravitational pull
our body was
no longer the book of bone
the detrimental predisposition
that took hold of us
in the depths
was now
luminous

the blunt soil, the turmoil

i screw
the turmoil
beside you until
our orbit
transmigrates
our synaptic
synastry
our horizontal
cosmology
our herbal literati
fuchsia it is
i turn the blunt soil
become mystical
black lineage
green sacrament i
screw it bitter
chop this earth
inside my mouth
where nothing
happens
other than
we happen
to fade

more poverty interwoven with equal happiness

they lived in a rented room
made of metal and want
more want than metal
a small box room
clear and bright
like the night wind
ascending the mountains
like the new moon's beams
the lightless light became a swaddle
the depression outlived all of them
& the home inside a boxcar
in the eyes of a child
became as opulent
as a magical tent
in a desert
dream
and
though
there was
no money
the joy
it grew
as air
and
{ }

for Levada Harris (1933–2000)

thirst is a way of knowing, not knowing

{ what } { i knew } { was pointless }
{ there on the river } { of some edge }

{ whose name } { i cannot speak }
{ was the alchemy } { of our existence }

{ inside our body } { a hollowness } { an aloofness }
{ so devout } { i began to call it } { holy }

{ how i glistened } { for no one } { other than myself }
{ how i became } { an outpouring } { for everyone }

                     { a cool drink of sorrow }
                     { laced with gold }

consider the dial

her voice were it   anything
other than a poem   inside
my solitude it would follow
me resound in me   without
any need for a record in our
ongoing general lucidity we
move from one body to the
next as if we have no   need
for bodies but to   simply
move and pass on   pass
through one orifice to   an-
other all by way of   sound
it's like an invisible group
of aunties   keep rotating a
dial and   as it turns our
world   disinters itself as
the dial moves   from gra-
vity to levity we exchange
our skins for others almost
as resplendent   as we last
wore them   but brighter
shades of cerulean   green
ochre black it's the   sound
of our voices the subtle nu-
ance in an inflection   how
it disintegrates on our   way
outside outside the wake of
all the marvel that is   black
consider our faces our skins
our old and new bodies and
no record of our   other
sounds other than what the
dial makes of it on a   scale
between dirt   and sky

a street in hollygrove

{ where each morning } { we open soft as sacrifice }

{ resolve once more } { to remain make again }

{ what meaning we cradle } { lose ourselves within it }

{ inside our side of a } { shotgun home }

    { is the memory of bulbancha }

{ black indigenous } { exhaust where we unravel }

{ beckon the light } { as if we were god }

    { hemming the wind }

        { as if time } { as if refusal }

{ to not step outside inside dispossession }

{ inside us is a glistening } { we cannot name }

    { too sacred to call it home }

angel of death

{ on the tip of an orifice } { her bruised green arousal }
        { her slow drag curvature }

{ across time and flesh } { drags us inside her torment }
        she weeps as she folds { fields as she unravels }

{ the wake of black music } { a yearning for green }
        an opening to spring { all by way of trap }

the inside stream dribbled and passed { back and forth
        between lovers } who touch each other

in the stacks { by way of sound } { all that unnecessary
        ingratiation to the idea of men }{ and women }

{ the dust who came } { before her } { inside her }
        she labors to fathom the unnecessary distance

{ between her departure } { miles between us }
        { she labors } { to get us off the page }

                { to get *off* }

homo ambrosia

in the black morning of baldwin
across the river in another country

a solemnity   a wretchedness
lulls the city

while the rest of you were sleeping
there was my human

dutiful supplicant
arrested in the night

a light in a darkened corridor

     the night prowls
as i had translated my body

for six hundred thousand years

in glacial want of a human
addicted   to the flesh

spirit of the times, the spirit of death

in the upper air unseen i lie
restless as the nocturne that did imagine me

      remember green's your color
      you are spring

i do not have to die today

the trees are half air
the texture of everything airs death

there is always a sound or color or feeling
in which i can arrive

{ the spirit of the depths }

green moves through
the out of trees
and grows

the way blue might want for green

      neptune i could sprint there

even though it is cold
i could sit there
breathe its lonely frequency

inhale its seductive lament

death comes by way of fragments
the word is no longer succulent

but *you are spring*
      you are spring
           you are spring

of being nameless

{ a man rages } { until he whistles } { on apricot street }
{ a woman rages } { as a man } { whistles his way off
the framework }

{ we listen as } { a wave burns } { inside these bodies }
{ beside ourselves } { we listen }
      { to a flame } { incite itself }

{ we the virtually faded signature } { play inside }
{ the long lineage } { of gravitation } { not play }
{ as much as squirm } { quiver our }
{ nervous impulse } { our chthonic ache }

      { to touch them on the inside part }
        { to call us by our name }

{ there is no name for us } { but them }
{ or us } { or we } { a collective drag }

      { a name we let go } { no sooner than
      our arrival } { on this cyan apparatus }
      { our saffron home } { we ruminate
      a quiet obsolescence } { we listen }
      { to the night } { as it tears }
      { waiting } { hungry at the seam }
      { for our new name } { our mythic
      congregation } { our origin }
      { our digression } { a grounds }

{ there is no word } { succulent } { erudite }
{ libidinous } { or haunt enough } { for our flesh }
{ as we wear it } { fluidly } { not nearly as old }
{ as we feel it } { brittle } { not divine as we hold it }

      { there is no name } { no known image }

{ we drag our bones } { in the long lineage of spite }
{ the rage inside the specter } { liquid heat }
{ you cannot see us as i am }

{ the lyric has gone black }

maroon choreography

To be made instrument, to be made implement, to be made that which hollows oneself out in order to be filled and to be hollowed out again and again, as in breath, as in spirit, as in *ruach*, as in Black *pneuma*. To be made instrument is to be made available for use, to be made instrument is to be made implement, to be made chamber, to be made something like a through line, a connection, a point of departure and a point of convergence. —Ashon T. Crawley, *The Lonely Letters*

if there is a collective ache, narrated by captive (incarcerated, bound, indebted) black people, detailing the various aches experienced within our black bodies, it is situated within our struggle to name our lives as sovereign, on our own terms, to demonstrate where and how and why we come outside, because to do so would defeat the effort in making a way out of no way, to do so could potentially eradicate our sovereignty. we know the tools are inadequate, those of us who live and read the philosophical lamentations (or is it laminations?) of black studies, who study blackness, who delve into the indigenous traditions, the spirituals, (non)performances of black life, inside and outside the afterlives of slavery, those many attempts, experiments in living as something otherwise. we know the attempts at training, the methods, are insufficient for the task of speaking, explaining, naming the ineffable. i began to think of (black) study and to study blackness in terms of breath, as in how the wind moves inside and outside the body, what air gives us. in quiet, while breathing in the dark, i began to understand the whole project of enslavement (also writing, also language, also money) and its afterlives, created a series of errant portals, a series of openings, a series of exits to exist outside. in the quiet, i sat and breathed in the sentient energy of all those former bodies (those temporary flesh realities) fleeing in the ephemerality of want. not documented, but felt inside the nonrational aperture of my hypersensory feeling. my work became a creative-intellectual practice of pneumatic cross-pollination. my intention was to cross-pollinate the single fields of our inherited thought procedures, because all my (and also our) laboring (field) ancestors arrived and tasked me with the responsibility to make a series of new fields, a nonfield, a *feels* space for our continued tarrying forth. i began with a series of ineffable questions on (black) social death, on trying to understand where black life is free (in the twenty-first century, now) to move outside the binary frameworks of public and private, free and captive, beyond the episteme of socialness (and sociality); as imagined and reimagined in various neoliberal capitalistic configurations of being together suspended in the wake of all that trauma of enslavement, of writing, of war, of money. because the choreographed apparatus of coloniality (and its vapid afterlives) had already offered a series of anticipated dance moves, had already designed a divided way of living one against the other, i wanted an achoreographic opening, a way of moving out and beyond and into. not a mimicked dance, an errant movement, not moved because some external apparatus has willed the body to move (through punishment, through force), but a progression of undulations (through trance, through transcendence). and, here, i mean movement/dance, quite literally in terms of how a body moves (alone, together, beside the apparatuses of coloniality), and also hauntologically in terms of what porous anteriority moves through a body, what worlds a body gains access to (is opened to) in movement. the bodies, the forms of all three poems emerged through deeply embodied, sensory, playful (meta-auditory) engagements with various works, with putting language to work, with forcing language against itself, with breaking language—breathing life back into it, locating an interior ambience. more than burrowing in, or jumping on, or following in the sound steps of those who came before me, i was (and remain) interested in the rhythm of enacting (queer)black radical traditions of breaking form and from, of making new forms derived from those prior fugitive movements undocumented as the wind. i began to formulate a method, a practice built in sustained slowness, suspension, ambience, aeration, and durational grief. not momentary suspension, a way of protracted slowness, refusal, refusing to return to a sense of *reality* (or realness), an extenuated pause, a refusal to participate in sociality. as i sought to break the record, i sent my body out as automata, moved around the world outside us in a trance. inside the depths of my deviant black interior, i drifted into the realms of unruliness. there is the concept of an audience, the onlooker, and then there is the band, or the swathe. i began to lose interest in the audience, and consider the imagined band, or more accurately the study group, i was drifting alongside, i was breathing in. i began to consider the unruliness i was summoned to participate in. i began to document that unruliness as a nonperformance. not choreographic, in the ontological captive sense of the written body, wayward in the paraontological sense of free movement as in unruly contemporary dancers who flail their bodies, shake the body off in undulation. i like to think contemporary dancers and choreographers taisha paggett, wayne mcgregor, honji wang, sébastian ramirez, and matthew gibbs practice unruly fugitive dances. their slow minimalist progressions, their practice of dance as translation (rather than reproduction), free the body from capture, from social death. taisha paggett's *a composite field* is an opening—they slowly drag their slumping body around a room, moving slow, alone, not in time with anything other than an invisible currency (the air composed by ambient musician yann novak). the way wayne mcgregor's dancers move in *autobiography*, sequentially in translation of his body, of his decoded blood, in perpetual undulation, in time with the sonic architecture of electronic artist jlin, is a way outside. in *monchichi*, honji wang and sébastian ramirez move alongside a solitary tree, as if the tree, the lone witness, the spirit of the tree, is what grants them permission to move. as freestyle dancer matthew gibbs undulates in a black ground, in *deeper*, his flesh disambiguates notation. the body of "recrudescence" first emerged through a single encounter—a conversation and an erotic mo(ve)ment i shared with a friend (whom i learned, after speaking with, i was already connected to through our shared connection with a friend) at a monthly underground queerblack zodiac dance party in new orleans called *ascen.dance*. designed by seven black and brown and indigenous humans, *ascen.dance* is a means of coming together, safely, with the intention of cultivating emotional and mental wellness in its attendants. for one saturday night each month, *ascen.dance* transforms cafe istanbul—a performance venue, bar, restaurant, and art gallery housed inside a larger healing center—into the wild unknown and summons the attendance of seven hundred (or more) people to dance. for the months and years after that encounter, i remained haunted by a poem whose air i caught wind of at one a.m., in a parking lot, in the breakout between dancing, when my friend began to talk about *queeribbeanness*. then again on the dance floor as our bodies moved together in time with a blurring of afrobeat, (liquid) r&b and soul, afrohouse, deep house, and jazz offered by a cluster of dj's, there was the beginning of a lyric that would haunt me for more than a year. as recrudescence grew from the fleeting encounter through which i heard its lament, i fell inside a crevasse—began to move inside (above and without) the errant spaces of before: the backwoods fugue, the juke joint, the hush arbors, all the unknown (unnamed) spaces curated by black indigenous people in the wild lushness of trees. as i expanded that transient human encounter i began to call in other sentient, porous, invisible interspecies life matter swirling outside us. as i carried around the life force of that poem inside me, i was also lost inside an entangled mass of poetry and works on climate change, mycelium, architecture, pranayama, astrology, jazz, dance, relation, history, and language. i was also thinking about histories of black (social) life and how black people, throughout time, have engaged in practices of communion and communing. what i was trying to make a way through, in the life of the poetic fragment of recrudescence, is the unrelenting gray of the city, the mood of the city, depression. caught inside the palimpsest of the backwoods, lost inside the city, i wanted to bring us back to the green of blackness, ease on down into the groove of the bottomsoil, slip inside the underground brilliance of mycelium, pull a lush feeling out from deep inside the earth, think about how people (now) come together outside the digital assistance of intermediary social media apparatuses. i was preoccupied with intimacy, relations between people, relations between all that exists. i began to ruminate on the possibility in coming together, to make friends (not followers) outside the strictures of surveillance. there was the

thought of our contemporary moment, of friendships, how
people come together in social death, and my general
sadness from my relentless search for a place to move, wild
into the sensuousness of the night, outside inside a groove,
outside the watchful eye of the mercantilist. i began to obsess
over finding a way outside surveillance, outside the market,
outside money. i began to question where people are free to
congregate without being hailed, without being appraised,
without being assigned a type of meaning, value, or category.
i wanted to get outside the nineteenth-century antebellum
market-driven impulse saidiya hartman describes where
(property) owners created dances where people could
come together with their own color, or kind, or type.
recrudescence is a metaphorical relevé, the up-and-down
progressions of general melancholia, a generational
malaise, prolonged across time, a feeling of giving up and
getting out. recrudescence is the anaphora, the repetitious
looping of long-overdue reparation. as i worked out
the eleven poetic fragments in "recrudescence," i
gradually eliminated the image of human bodies, so what is
left is a muted happening, or a series of oscillations—
absence and presence, abstraction and expansion, transience
and sentience. i held on to a question, a series of questions,
about the rise and fall, the recurrences within intimate
relationships, how relationships change as everything outside
changes. i began to focus on what else exists between people
who come together, not the tangible, short-lived flesh
realities, but the opaque expanse, the murky unknown,
how intimacy connects everything and everyone. this
fixation on the shift between what is known and the secret
space of the unknown, i began to think of as an erotic
cosmopsychosomatic surround in the air of recrudescence,
because this is the feeling it offered me as i wrote it. the
stars-body-spores, all together in a dance that lasts beyond
the physical exchange between two people. i fell inside
the depths of a moment, hung out there, in the slickness
of joy, came out someplace else. but the matter of this
poem was never really concerned with my person. this

isn't about me. the invisible dancers in these poems stole away to a secret dance, in the trees, beside the river. in the air of the twenty-first century, in the recrudescence of the swamp, in the air of our other century (cosmic) kin, what worlds do we all have access to as we flail our bodies deep into the night? i became fixated on tracing how the transcendent ones—living and dead—show up to help us, those of us still cast on earth and in the ground, to move away and move outside this simulation as it holds us. i began to search for something more than flesh, for something more than possible, for an opening. there is always a familiar sonic frequency, an air i cannot get outside, an addiction to a bodiless drift as it holds me, as it moves me up in motion. sometimes it is the fragrance of some inexpressible memory of a lover, other times it is the tempestuous music of a mood, a cycle i cannot stop looping (for hours, days, years at a time). then "porous aftermath," the fugue—the contrapuntal composition, the flight. if recrudescence is a fragmented mood of a city, then porous aftermath is the lingering sensation of the feeling as it existed before the city, what never left (even as it was destroyed to make the city). porous aftermath began with the thought of the histories of pre- and postcolonial southern louisiana. in the residual swamp of contemporary southern louisiana, the air is moist and heavy. we are all haunted by blackness that never left, what has never found rest, what lingers in bulbancha (the indigenous name for what is now new orleans). i was searching for an opening (a furtive way outside) when i began to see dancers, inside the trees, the energy of dancers. where i was living in the palimpsest of country, in an ill-designed suburban city in the south, on its way to becoming a city, i was suspended inside the feeling of before. then i proceeded to fall inside the earth. how i got there? i used my imagination. on a summer walk in rural louisiana with a friend, we slipped inside the wild open secret of the marsh. as we moved in silence, inside the green and blue and pink and yellow and white and red earth around us, the slick moisture of the earth pulled us deep inside a fecund tree line.

as the earth commenced to swallow us, we fell outside and into. there was the land as we saw it, the trace of so much want in the air between us, as we felt it, tasted it, and smelled it. all this wild earth, untouched, unknown, alone. in the air of those trees on the other side of highway 44, i fell into an opening that was memory, lost all sense of who or what i thought i was before. what i had been reading about, for years, in historical works, creative works, philosophical works—about black people's fraught histories with colonial languages (with naming, with communing, with writing, with being known)—all of it was upended in a single walk into trees, into wildness. then on the other side of a ridge, on the other side of train tracks, on that same day, we found a cane field. we sat alone before the canebrake, mostly in silence, inside our car, staring at compacted rows of earth on one side, a tiny tract of manufactured homes on the other. we sat in our car, inebriated as the air, caught up in shared illumination. we were before the earth, before run, before ruin, before escape and constant escape, together. we began to talk about an energy of the earth, a spirit of the swamp, a feeling of divine restlessness, a succulence of sound in the air of rural blackness. the form of porous aftermath, its haltingly staccato undulation, is a recursive preoccupation with the word *not* (as in refusal) with moving outside nominal predisposition. porous aftermath tries to get there, to that negative space, to the unnamable space of blackness, by refusing to participate in naming rituals (and associations) of property. i think of the thirty-three geometric configurations that make up porous aftermath as the remnants of some contraband sensation, left over by a wandering group of seven, carrying out (and on and through) a roomless ritual as it once took place in the trees, a timeless signature of the wind. i had been thinking about space, for years, the nature of objects and subjects within a particular enclosure, a container, or room. inside the trees, inside the swamp, inside the memory of black indigenous life, i started to question the myth of black life as we know it (or think we know it) in the context of the united states. what invisible porous movements did those (indigenous, timeless) black people who moved outside the (sixteenth- and seventeenth-century agrarian) framework, out there in the breath of those trees we came into, leave behind simply by way of air? i began to think of the air around us as an ongoing shape lineage of refusal. torkwase dyson calls the historical shapes black bodies create in space *fugitive shapes, hypershapes, abstraction*. i began to think of air as a fugitive abstraction. as i worked through porous aftermath, i thought about the unseen shapes, the unseen languages, held over in the pneumatic fugitive trace of all that beauty, all that struggle, experienced by black people who had been enslaved in seventeenth-century louisiana, who escaped and lived with the trees in the swamp, whose abysmal abyssal breath flows within me, too, because i live here, because i am open, because i receive its energy, attempt to give it form. what i had been trying to understand about the air came through in the bodies of these poems, in mostly minimalist abstraction. "nocturnal work" derives its name from carl jung's *the red book / liber novus*, a creative, esoteric account of his ontological break, or blackness, and his attempt to delve into the interior of his personal unconsciousness, his trauma, his depths. nocturnal work is the name jung gives to his secret nightly work to reconcile a tension between his diurnal self (or the "i") and his divine nocturnal self (or soul). though i did not feel the same split or tension as carl jung, i had been wading around, lost inside the opacity of my black interior, deeply invested in a type of shadow work of my own before the life of nocturnal work brought me, unwittingly, to carl jung's *liber novus*. i had been struggling to write "nocturnal work," until it named itself, which is a little ironic in the sense so much of the work in this collection is concerned with getting outside naming rituals. but like i said, the poem named itself. after the poem announced itself, the rest of it arrived as a type of wandering cento poem, composed of fragments from other poems and the unspoken feeling in instrumental songs, or the air. there was my grief, a twenty-year ache, shadow. my first love and spiritual teacher was my grandma, levada. levada—who mastered the quiet (sovereign) art of doing nothing other than sitting outside, in prolonged silence, looking and listening but not speaking—taught me meditation, taught me stillness. how to *steal away*, as stillness. what grandma knew, because she could not read and write, was how to move with the ease of inner knowing. levada's voice, her sensual speech, was an erotics, a sonic delight, a rural departure from how people sounded in southern california around me when i was a child. it was not so much her accent as her timing, her syntax, her deep pauses, her quiet. not silenced, intentionally quiet. i was never overwhelmed by her voice, to the point of disinterest, and because she was not loud, i began to wait for her utterance, eager to hear, again, her slow creep, to make entire worlds out of the lingering texture of some faraway place she held in her throat, a syntax that was divinely aural black and oral and intimate. that she only had a relationship with this language by way of sound might have explained her reticence. that she was inherently spiritual might have explained the rest of it. levada was a living poem, though she could not write a poem. in memory of my grandmother, i stole away inside these lines, in stillness, to form the twenty-two individual poems of nocturnal work. or, i could say nocturnal work was quilted together as a series of fragments from other works. while writing nocturnal work i was also attempting to document a sonic progression of grief, to move through my own black shadow, to write through personal grief, to carry grief outside myself, listen to it. i aerated the grounds i inherited until i could reemerge an aspect of air. there were many musical accompaniments (alice coltrane, emahoy tsegué-maryam guèbrou, sun ra, flying lotus, hiroshi yoshimura, steve reich) to help me write this restless section, this section that almost refused to be written, but pauline oliveros's *deep listening* ("suiren" on repeat, all day, every day, for a few weeks) finally called it out. the wavelike curvature, paired with the block formations of the twenty-two individual poems in nocturnal work, possibly offers a visual portrayal of the sound of my grandmother's lost voice, how it might have modulated— maybe even blocked itself, at times—if i had a recording that i were able to translate into an image, but there is no recording, only memory. all three poems, "recrudescence," "porous aftermath," and "nocturnal work," consider processes of losing the body, of communing, of getting outside and lingering there. to will a body, or a series of bodies, to move together, in time with nothing other than the energy of a moment, or an invisible affect, is a way of communicating beyond capture. this dance, an open dance, what i have begun to think of as a wild, anachoreographic opening, is the type of movement that wills the body upside fear. this anachoreographic opening, a slow, minimalist dance, an unruly dance, a dance of duration, is how i imagine the invisible dancers in *maroon choreography* move. i could say, i kept coming back to an underground room where transcendent bodies gathered in symbiosis and together we undulated freely. i could say it was a room made of wind and we all cross-pollinated each other. i tremble with the sensations moving outside me. what lingers in the air outside me, and what lingers in these poems, is a black indigenous undercurrent, a tantric sensation of coming. or at least this is how i move in it. the air outside me, the tremulous wake of ecstasy, surrenders to gravity, strengthens itself in shadow, touches me at midnight. since childhood, i am compelled by an invisible current, a somnambulist want that calls me in the night. the air moves, my body rises up in wait. no one is there to see it, though it does happen :: each night, i dance, alone, at midnight. not for anyone's amusement but my own. i surrender to the opaque present, read another book, expand my synesthetic sense, get outside my body. body as in flesh, as in narrative, as in governance, as in myth, as in binary, as in ego, as in law, as in record, as in limitation. when i am deep inside my body i am also wandering far outside my body, curious to find the words i still do not have to describe a continuum between social death and asociality. i was gone for seven years while working on this book. the first four years, i spent time reading. then for three more years, i continued reading as i slowly wrote these poems. if i had not been listening, if i had not had the good sense to write the poems down as they came, i might have missed a chance to form something from nothing. at the end of this, all i have is a stronger practice, a clearer sense of where i exist in relation to everything and nothing. i study. i move. i open. i have nothing else. no resolutions, no answers. ruin all around us, there is no rest—but friendship amongst the pneumatic ones, the airy ones, the forest ones. for those of us who never find the privilege of rest are free to fade into porous aftermath, become orgiastic wind, dance out of nothing, become nothing, become all.

C. Riley Snorton   *Black on Both Sides:*
Saidiya Hartman   *Scenes of Subjection*
Fred Moten   *In the Break*   *Black and Blur*
Ann Cvetkovich   *Depression*
Gaston Bachelard   *The Psychoanalysis of Fire*

A Racial History of Trans Identity

Lose Your Mother   *Wayward Lives, Beautiful Experiments*

Stolen Life   *Universal Machine*

An Archive of Feelings

Intuition of the Instant   *Poetics of Space*   *Air and Dreams*

Feel Trio

The Little Edges

Fred Moten

Sarah Jane Cervenak *Wandering*

Daphne Brooks *Bodies in Dissent*

Neil Roberts *Freedom as Marronage*

Richard Iton *In Search of a Black Fantastic*

Kevin Quashie *The Sovereignty of Quiet*

consent not to be a single being

Boy with Thorn

Rickey Laurentiis

coda

Fred Moten

Dionne Brand   *Ossuaries*   *The Blue Clerk*   *An Autobiography of*

Christina Sharpe   *In the Wake*   Kimberly Brown

André Breton   *Manifestoes of Surrealism*

Édouard Glissant   *Poetics of Relation*   *Poetic Intention*

Simone Browne   *Dark Matters*   Katherine McKittrick   *Demonic Grou*

Sylvia Wynter: On Being Human as Praxis

American Canon

Dear Angel of Death

Simone White   *Of Being Dispersed*   Nathaniel Mackey   *Blue Fasa*

coda

...tobiography of Reading

The Repeating Body

L'amour Fou

R. A. Judy *(Dis)Forming the*

Sentient Flesh

Splay Anthem

Nod House

Solimar Otero *Archives of Conjure: Stories of the Dead in Afrola*

Hortense Spillers   *Black, White, and in Color*   Kara Keeling   *The Witch's Fl*

L. K. Gill

Dub

Jennifer C. N

M Archive

Spill

Alexis Pauline Gumbs

coda

Cultures

    Queer Times, Black Futures

        Erotic Islands   LaMonda Horton-Stallings   *Funk the Erotic*

            The Black Body in Ecstasy

                M. NourbeSe Philip *She Tries Her Tongue, Her Silence Softly Breaks*

Karen Barad — *Meeting the Universe Halfway* — Donna J. Haraway

Anna Lowenhaupt Tsing (and friends) *Arts of Living on a*

Anna Lowenhaupt Tsing — *The Mushroom at the End of*

Mel Y. Chen — *Animacies* — Jane Bennett

Kathryn Yusoff — *A Billion Black*

Ed Roberson — To See the Earth Before the End of the World

Staying with the Trouble

Damaged Planet (Ghosts/Monsters)

the World

Vibrant Matter

Anthropocenes or None

Trophic Cascade

Camille T. Dungy

Taylor Johnson

Inheritance

M. NourbeSe Philip *Zong!* Brenda Marie Osbey *In These Houses* *All Saints* *All Souls* Carolyn Rodgers *The Heart as Evergreen* *Fictions of the Land and Flesh* Cathy Che *Split* Deleuze *Difference and Repetition* Slavery's Exiles Justin Phillip Reed *Indecency* Danielle Vogel *Between Grammars* Jenny Xie *Eye Level* Heather Christle *The Trees, The Trees* Franny Choi *Soft Science* Judith Butler *Bodies That Matter* *Undoing Gender* *Senses of the Subject* Notes toward a Performative Theory of Assembly Sebastian Clark "Sun & Flesh" Ashon T. Crawley *Blackpentecostal Breath* *The Lonely Letters* Gwendolyn Hall *Africans in Colonial Louisiana* Jack Halberstam *In a Queer Time and Place* *The Queer Art of Failure* Being Time Susan Howe *Debths* *The Nonconformist's Memorial* Terrance Hayes *Hip Logic* *Wind in a Box* *How to Be Drawn* *American Sonnets for My Past and Future Assassin* Nicole Terez Dutton *If One of Us Should Fall* Ted Joans *Black Pow-Wow* Jenny Johnson *In Full Velvet* Maggie Nelson *Bluets* Sharon Olds *Odes* Bob Kaufman *Solitudes Crowded by Loneliness* Fred Moten *All That Beauty* Yanyi *Year of Blue Water* Laura Mullen *After I Was Dead* Dawn Lundy Martin *Discipline* Good Stock Strange Blood A Gathering of Matter / A Matter of Gathering Eileen Myles *Not Me* Nathanaël *Je Nathanaël* Diana Taylor *Performance* Cole Swensen *On Walking On*

Michelle Wright *Physics of Blackness*

Kathleen Stewart *Ordinary Affects*

Sharon Olds The Dead and the Living

Kathleen Stewart & Lauren Berlant *The Hundred*

Eve Kosofsky Sedgwick *Touching Feeling*

Stephanie E. Smallwood *Saltwater Slavery*

Elizabeth Alexander *The Black Interior*

taisha paggett "vestibular mantra" M. NourbeSe Philip "Black w/holes"

Karma-Glin-Pa *The Tibetan Book of the Dead*

Jack Goody *The Logic of Writing and the Organization of Society*

Carl Phillips Wild Is the Wind

Lara Glenum

Robin Coste Lewis *Voyage of the Sable Venus*

Susan Sontag *Against Interpretation*

Matthew Gibbs "Deeper"

Elaine Scarry *The Body in Pain*

Rebecca Solnit *A Field Guide to Getting Lost*

Daniel Sayers *A Desolate Place for a Defiant People*

Lawrence Powell *The Accidental City*

Gayatri Gopinath *Unruly Visions*

All Hopped Up on Fleshy Dum Dums

C. G. Jung The Red Book / Liber Novus

The Psychology of Kundalini Yoga E. Patrick Johnson

José Esteban Muñoz Cruising Utopia Disidentificatio

André Lepecki Singularities LaRhonda

Amber Musser Sensual Excess

Tavia Nyong'o Afro-Fabulations

Malidoma Patrice Somé

Layli Long Soldier Whereas

Ocean Vuong Night Sky with Exit Wounds

coda

Evie Shockley *the new black*   *semiautomatic*

Archetypes and the Collective Unconscious

(and friends) *No Tea, No Shade*

Tiffany Lethabo King *The Black Shoals*

Manigault-Bryant *Talking to the Dead*

Timothy Morton *Dark Ecology*

Jessica Krug *Fugitive Modernities*

Of Water and the Spirit

André Lepecki *Exhausting Dance*
Mark Rifkin *Fictions of Land and Flesh*

Mark Rifkin *Beyond Settler Time*

Édouard Glissant *Poétique de la Relation* Reina Gossett *Trap Door*

Joshua Beckman *The Lives of the Poems*

Henry Dumas "Thalia"

Gabrielle Commander *Afro-Atlantic Flight*

Michelle Calvocoressi *Rocket Fantastic*

D. Goldman *I Want to Be Ready*
Kai Green "Troubling the Waters" Consciously
Sondra Fraleigh (and friends) Moving Consciously

K. Dowman *Masters of Mahamudra*

Marisa Fuentes *Dispossessed Lives* Nicole Fleetwood *Troubling Vision*

Alexis De Veaux *Yabo*   *Blue Heat*

Pauline Oliveros (and friends) *Deep Listening*

Jlin "Soundtrack for Wayne McGregor's *Autobiography*"

taisha paggett *The antique Blacks* / *Theography*

Flying Lotus *Cosmogramma*

Alice Coltrane *Journey in Satchidananda* / *World Galaxy*

Sun Ra *Fireside Chat with Lucifer*

Yann Novak *The Future Is a Forward Escape*

A Composite Field
Moses Sumney   *Græ*   *Aromanticism*

Wayne McGregor *Chroma* *Autobiography*

Flamagra

Honji Wang & Sébastien Ramirez *Monchichi*

The Extractive Zone   *Exhausting Dance*   *Sonic Intimacy*   *Black Madness*
The World We Have   *After The Party*
Trans*   *Necropolitics*   *The Roots of Tantra*
                                                   Making Dances That Matter
                                                   Braiding Sweetgrass

Maroon Societies   *Parenthetical Hinge*   *Sensing Sound*
       Unthinking Mastery   *The Sorrow and the Fast of It*
"*Black Performance Theory*"   *Dark Memories*

If the work were beside itself it might help us understand something about refusal - Were it experimental the unforeseeable production call it art - *yes art as research and research as art* - Poetics - Insinuate renewal - After something flat like - in the fifteenth century the printing press papered bodies the property stationers published bodies - The dominating storied circumstance of our being here together as paper - Then something crude - fuck lineage

{ **black study**, poiēsis }

Somewhere succulent and hush - { beside } - some bodies stole and spread out leveled into - If you are looking for a way into somewhere else then move horizontally - Sprawl out anagrammatic of the underneath - A black field a horizon - An experiment in taking leave leave taking stealing - Away is a process of coming upside - *art i have no idea* - If a group of people fade out in the black morning what becomes of all that mourning

{ **black study**, paraontology }

We touch in distance - Nocturnal visits as lovers - Sentient flesh - Exposed and underexposed to everything and nothing - Ligature - A bass line scrawls from one end of a root network from one end of a mycelial filament to the base of a cypress tree - Hyperbolic in the copse - Wayward in the wood shed - An infinite line tunnels its way through mud brings us back to magic city - We never touch let alone beside the forest - We dance inside a blue hand - Then dance a dance for timeless time everywhere and nowhere beside ourselves antiphonal asymptotic

{ **black study**, geometries }

Call it cosmic anindex call it nonperformance the way we live upside land - *is it paraontological yet* - Black study - call us out - Outside the book a memory - Beside want a language - *will i tell you about it* - *No* - If you know you know - *so i went back in more than myself* - As hyperbola two or three figures scrawl underneath the topsoil tunnel from one end of our cosmic collective intimacy to the other - Almost touching and not - Our chthonic cousins - Our contortionist kin - Each opening another portal - *come play with me* - fuck gender { dig me } out and out and also gone - blue as green as dust

{ **black study**, refusal }

Cousin tree or lover tree - Our commonness common sense what we hold in common - Oracle tree - The book desires - The book has need :: to shed in public :: Wooden mimesis - A saxophone on a highway - A poet prostrate beside a clock - debt - Rune a run :: (0,0) :: a center { ~~missing equation~~ } slips from one run to the next never gains any time in its flesh for all the time in the bottomsoil - Excess - Or blackness has a way of renewing in the wake of all that death - As bodilessness borderlessness loneliness - *Loss* is a way of loving - As hyphae cue a curve as I as we as they - We love each other in quiet - *is it fleshless yet* - distant touch - is it - you know - public woodshed wet

{ **black study**, tautology }

Dancers on and in the ground unseen - Hush - bought and sold spirit bought and sold the word - Not bought and sold stole themselves in blackness and sometimes they come up as cypress knees a quilt or a black artist - In the lush heart as evergreen on and in the ground - nonsense - Not money - Not owned - Not possessed - *is it an ontological break yet* - Loop go back and break it - Go back and shout it - Glimmer as our elder trees remind us to glimmer - *is it black study yet*

{ **black study**, hush arbors }

Build a universal machine and dance in it - trans*m*utate it - Practice so you can move it - Put sequins on it - Call it practice - Slow rehearsal it - Global drag it - Tuneless and impotent - Run it - The futurepresent continuation of - *also also and and also also* - ring shout out the now - *poetry* - not kill a tree *not not not* property not and also - global blackness - Open a door - Adore it - The anindex - Aerate it as a { } does - A bald cypress - Tremble with it - Stir it up - Whine - Meet us in the copse or open field - Trouble air - *so write a theory about how you might can't index this* - praise break

    And breathe

                                                   { **black study**, our mutual air }

www.ingramcontent.com/pod-product-compliance
Lightning Source LLC
Chambersburg PA
CBHW050554160426
43199CB00015B/2659